The 2nd RAFFI Songbook

42 SONGS FROM RAFFI'S ALBUMS
BABY BELUGA, RISE AND SHINE
and ONE LIGHT, ONE SUN.

Piano arrangements by
Catherine Ambrose

Design and illustration by
Joyce Yamamoto

CROWN PUBLISHERS, INC.   NEW YORK

ACKNOWLEDGEMENTS

Many thanks to Catherine Ambrose for her delightfully musical piano arrangements. She took great care to preserve the spirit of the recorded songs, and also made the suggestions for rhythm accompaniment.

Thanks also to Ken Whiteley for his advice, and to Avis Romm for her generous assistance.

Special thanks to Joyce Yamamoto whose joyful illustrations dance with the music.

Consultation services by McCalla Design Associates.

Back cover photo by David Street.

Music engraving and typesetting by Musictype Limited, Goodwood, Ontario.

Library of Congress Cataloging-in-Publication Data

Raffi.
  [Songs. Selections]
  The 2nd Raffi songbook.

  Summary: A collection of forty-two songs from previous albums by the noted Canadian recording artist.
  1. Children's songs. [1. Songs] I. Ambrose, Catherine. II. Yamamoto, Joyce, ill. III. Second Raffi songbook. IV. Raffi songbook.
  M1997.R1726R32   1987   87-75-0546
  ISBN 0-517-56638-9   784.624

  10 9 8 7 6 5 4 3 2   /MH

CONTENTS

BABY BELUGA

Baby Beluga . . . . .7 -1
Biscuits in the Oven 9
Oats and Beans and Barley .13
Day O 15
Thanks A Lot 19
To Everyone in All the World 21
All I Really Need 23
Over In The Meadow 27
This Old Man 29
Kumbaya 31
Morningtown Ride 33

RISE AND SHINE

Rise and Shine 35
Walk, Walk, Walk 37
Thumbelina 41
Wheels on the Bus 43
Daniel 45
Five Little Ducks 47
He's Got the Whole World 48
Big Beautiful Planet 50
I'm in the Mood 52
Something in My Shoe 55
Michaud 57
Tete, Epaules 59
Let's Do the Numbers Rumba 60
Ducks Like Rain 62
Row, Row, Row 64
This Little Light of Mine 65

ONE LIGHT, ONE SUN

Time to Sing 67
Apples and Bananas 70
Take Me Out to the Ballgame 72
Octopus's Garden 75
Fais Dodo 77
In My Garden 79
Riding in an Airplane 81
Like Me and You 84
Down on Grandpa's Farm 87
The Bowling Song 89
Tingalayo 92
Walk Outside 94
De Colores 96
Twinkle, Twinkle, Little Star .99
One Light, One Sun 100

Notes to Keyboard Players 102
Notes to Guitar Players 102
Index 104

Baby Beluga

With a gentle bounce

Words and music by Raffi and D. Pike

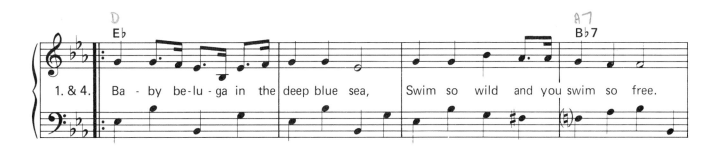

1. & 4. Ba - by be-lu - ga in the deep blue sea, Swim so wild and you swim so free.

Last time to Coda

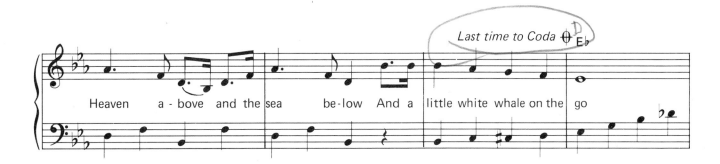

Heaven a - bove and the sea be-low And a little white whale on the go

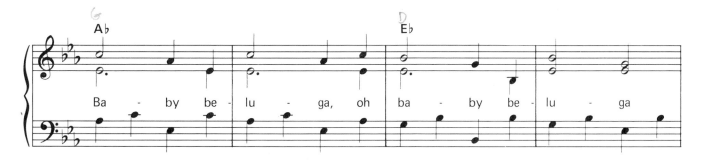

Ba - by be-lu - ga, oh ba - by be-lu - ga

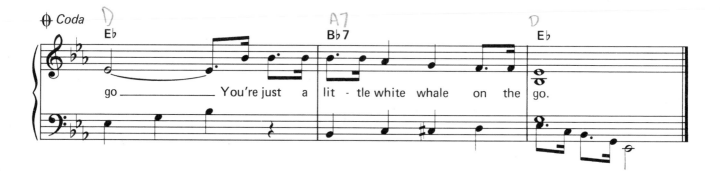

2. Way down yonder where the dolphins play,
   Where you dive and splash all day
   Waves roll in and the waves roll out.
   See the water squirtin' out of your spout.

   > Baby beluga, oh baby beluga,
   > Sing your little song; sing for all your friends.
   > We like to hear you.

3. When it's dark, you're home and fed,
   Curl up snug in your water bed
   Moon is shining and the stars are out.
   Good night, little whale, good night.

   > Baby beluga, oh baby beluga,
   > With tomorrow's sun, another day's begun.
   > You'll soon be waking.

 To play and sing this song in the Key of E as Raffi does, place a capo behind the
2nd fret and substitute the chords

	D	A7	E	G
for	E♭	B♭7	F	A♭

Biscuits in the Oven

Words and music by Bill Russell

Brightly

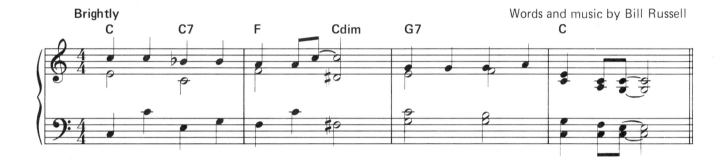

Chorus

Bis - cuits in the ov - en gon - na watch 'em rise, Bis - cuits in the ov - en gon - na

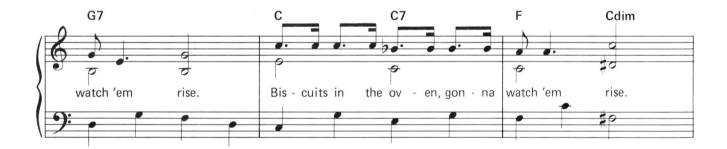

watch 'em rise. Bis - cuits in the ov - en, gon - na watch 'em rise.

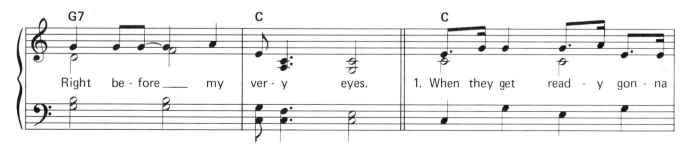

Right be - fore ___ my ver - y eyes. 1. When they get read - y gon - na

jump and shout, When they get read-y gon-na jump and shout

When they get read-y gon-na jump and shout, Roll my eyes ___ and

INTERLUDE

bug them out. Hey hey!

2. Gon-na clap my hands and stomp my feet, ___

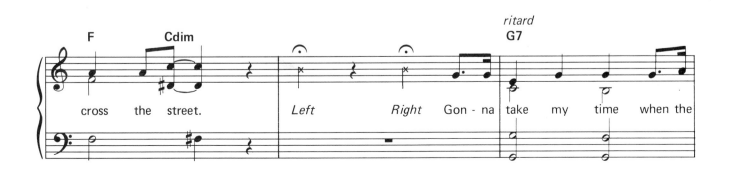

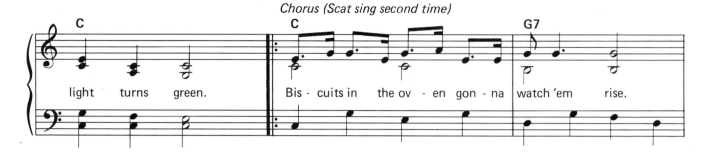

light turns green. Bis - cuits in the ov - en gon - na watch 'em rise.

Bis - cuits in the ov - en, gon - na watch 'em rise. Bis - cuits in the ov - en gon - na

2nd time to Coda

watch 'em rise, Right be - fore____ my ver - y eyes.

CODA

(Scat singing)

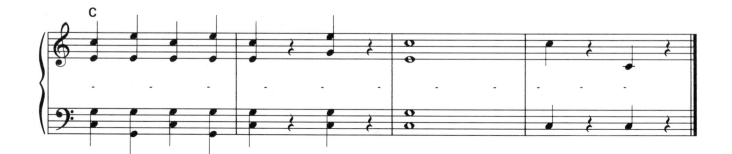

Oats and Beans and Barley

Sprightly

Traditional

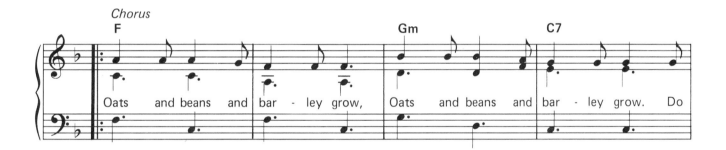

Chorus

Oats and beans and bar - ley grow, Oats and beans and bar - ley grow. Do

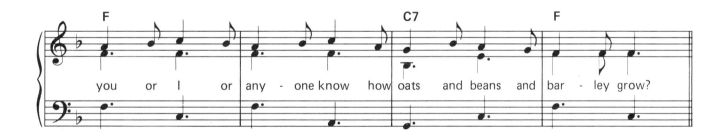

you or I or any - one know how oats and beans and bar - ley grow?

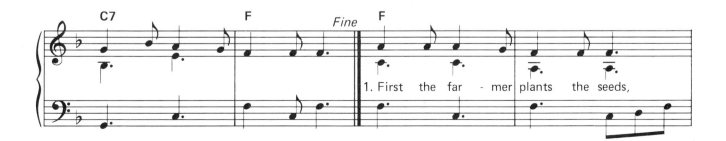

Fine

1. First the far - mer plants the seeds,

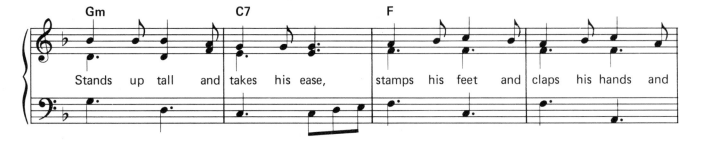

Stands up tall and takes his ease, stamps his feet and claps his hands and

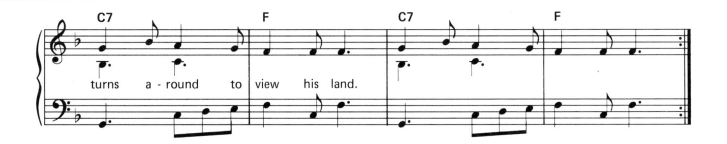

turns a - round to view his land.

2. Then the farmer waters the ground
Watches the sun shine all around
Stamps his feet and claps his hands
And turns around to view his land.

To play this with the chords of the Key of D,
substitute the chords   D | Em | A7
for   F | Gm | C7
Capo behind the 3rd fret brings you to the Key of F.

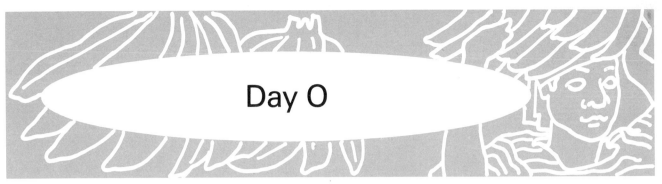

Day O

Traditional

Day - o mis-sa day - o Day-light come and me wan go home,

Day - o mis-sa day - o Day-light come and me wan go home,

Work all night 'til the morn-in' come Day-light come and me wan go home.

Stack ba-nan-a 'til the morn-in' come Day-light come and me wan go home.

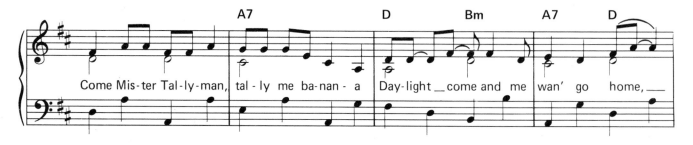

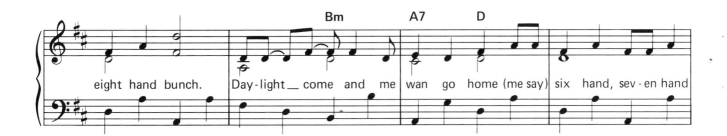

Thanks A Lot

Words & music by Raffi

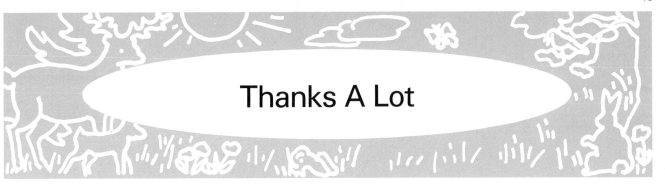

Gently

1. Thanks a lot,   Thanks for the sun in the

sky,   Thanks a lot.

Thanks for the clouds so___ high._____

2. Thanks a lot
   Thanks for the whispering wind
   Thanks a lot
   Thanks for the birds in the spring

3. Thanks a lot
   Thanks for the moonlit night
   Thanks a lot
   Thanks for the stars so bright

4. Thanks a lot
   Thanks for the wonder in me
   Thanks a lot
   Thanks for the way I feel

5. Thanks for the an - i - mals | Thanks for the land | Thanks for the peo-ple ev - ery- | where.

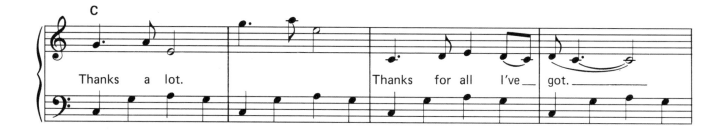

Thanks   a   lot.   Thanks   for   all   I've__   got._____

Thanks   for   all__ I've__   got._____

 Raffi plays this with the capo behind the 3rd fret. His forefinger bars the first 4 strings behind the 2nd fret, leaving the pinkie and other fingers for melody. Thumb of the right hand plays an alternating bass while the fingers pick the melody. For easy accompaniment, strum the C chord once in every bar (no capo needed).

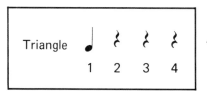

To Everyone in All the World

Traditional

Brightly

1. To

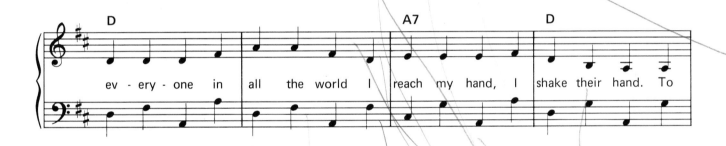

ev - ery - one in all the world I reach my hand, I shake their hand. To

ev - ery - one in all the world I shake my hand like this.

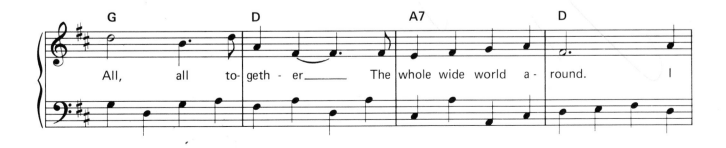

All, all to - geth - er_____ The whole wide world a - round. I

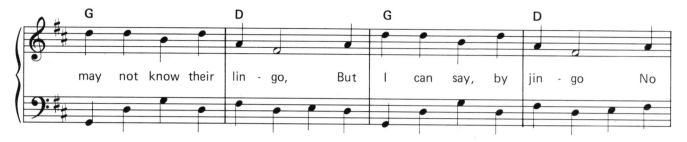

may not know their lin - go, But I can say, by jin - go No

mat - ter where you live, We can shake hands.

2. À tous et chacun dans le monde
   Je tends la main, je l'eur donne la main
   À tous et chacun dans le monde
   Je donne la main comme ça
   Tous tous ensemble au monde entier je chante
   C'est très facile entre humains
   Avec une poignée de main
   N'importe où dans le monde on peut s'entendre

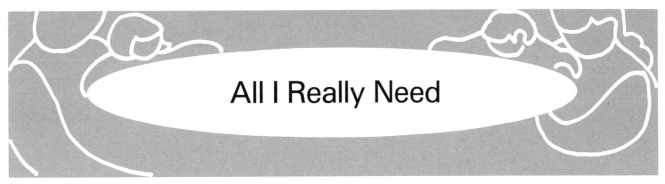

All I Really Need

Words & music by Raffi
D. Pike and B. & B. Simpson

song in my heart, ____ love in my fam - i - ly. ____

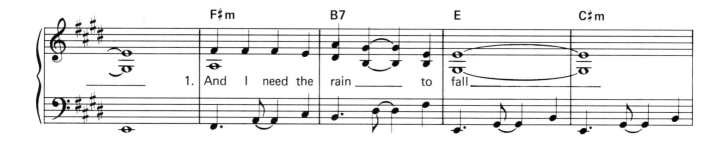

____ 1. And I need the rain ____ to fall ____

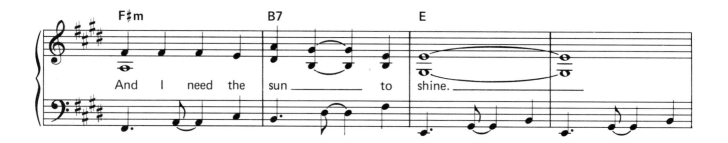

And I need the sun ____ to shine. ____

To give life to the seeds we sow. To give the food we need to grow.

All I real - ly need ___ is a song in my heart ___

and love in my fam - i - ly. ___

℅ *Chorus*

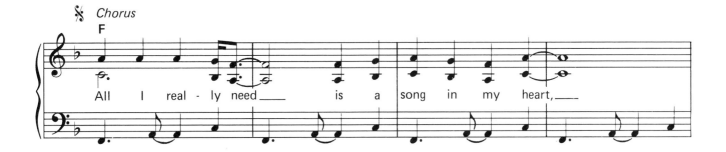

All I real - ly need ___ is a song in my heart, ___

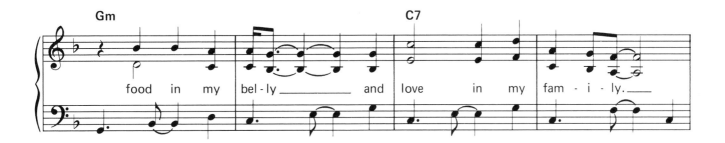

food in my bel - ly ___ and love in my fam - i - ly. ___

All I real - ly need ___ is a song in my heart. ___

* Repeat from here to Fine for fade ending, 2nd time.

love in my fam - i - ly. ___

2. And I need some clean wa-ter for drink-in'._____

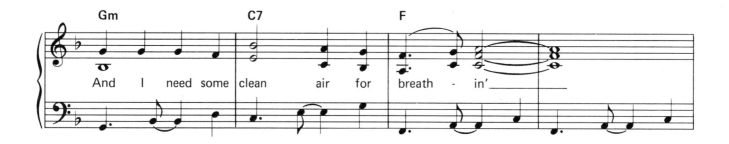

And I need some clean air for breath-in'_____

So that I _____ can grow up strong, Take my place where I be-long.___

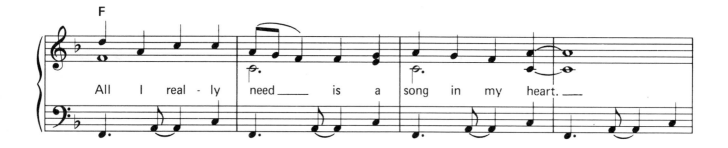

All I real-ly need_____ is a song in my heart.___

and love in my fam-i-ly._____

Over In The Meadow

Traditional
Adapted lyrics by Lee Hays and Doris Kaplan

Merrily

1. O-ver in the mead-ow in a

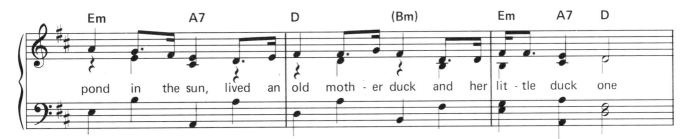

pond in the sun, lived an old moth-er duck and her lit-tle duck one

"__" said the moth-er, "__" said the one And they quacked and were hap-py in their

pond in the sun.

2. Over in the meadow in a stream so blue
   Lived an old mother fish and her little fish two
   "__" said the mother, "__"__" said the two
   And they swam and were happy in the stream so blue.

3. Over in the meadow in a nest in a tree
   Lived an old mother bird and her birdies three
   "__" said the mother, "__ __ __" said the three
   And they sang and were happy in their nest in the tree.

4. Over in the meadow on a rock by the shore.
   Lived an old mother frog and her little frogs four
   "__" said the mother, "__ __ __ __" said the four
   And they croaked and were happy on the rock by the shore.

5. Over in the meadow in a big bee hive
   Lived an old mother bee and her little bees five
   "__" said the mother, "__ __ __ __ __" said the five
   And they buzzed and were happy in the big bee hive.

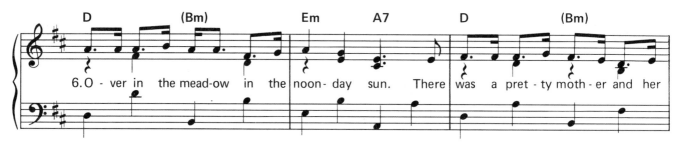

6. O - ver in the mead-ow in the noon-day sun. There was a pret-ty moth-er and her

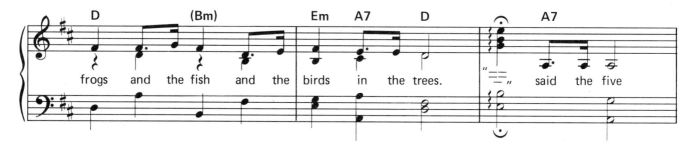

ba - by one. "Lis - ten" said the moth-er "to the ducks and the bees, To the

frogs and the fish and the birds in the trees. "__" said the five

"__" said the four "__" said the three "__" said the two "__" said the one, And the

lit - tle ba - by laughed just to hear such fun.

This Old Man

Traditional
Adapted by Raffi, D. Pike, B. & B. Simpson

With a blues feel

1. This old man, he plays one, He plays one on his old drum, Oh

yes, yes, yes, uh ___ huh

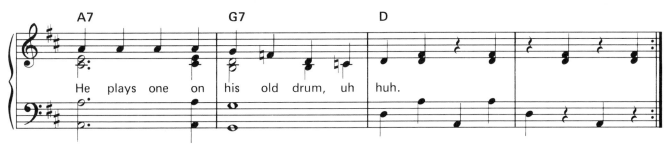

He plays one on his old drum, uh huh.

2. This old man, he plays two . . . . on his kazoo

3. This old man, he plays three . . . on his ukelele

4. This old man, he plays four . . . . on his guitar

5. This old man, he plays five . . . . with his friend Clive

CODA

This old man, he plays __ one. This old man, he plays __ two
This old man, he plays __ three, This old man, he plays __ four.

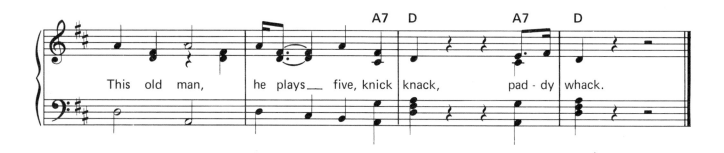

This old man, he plays __ five, knick knack, pad - dy whack.

Raffi worked out this bluesy adaptation on the guitar in the Key of E, pinching the 3rd note of the E (1st) string. To play in E,

substitute chords E | B7 | A7

for D | A7 | G7

Kumbaya

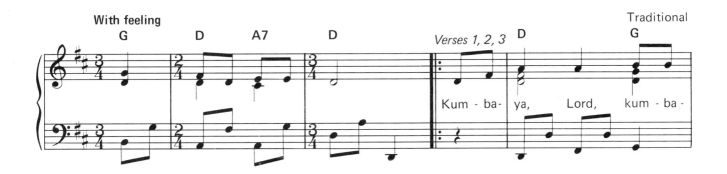

2. Someone's praying, Lord, kumbaya

3. Someone's crying', Lord, kumbaya

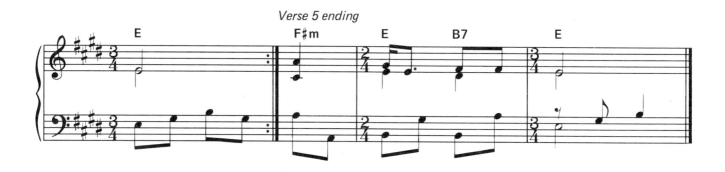

4. Someone's singing, Lord, kumbaya

5. Kumbaya, Lord, kumbaya

Morningtown Ride

Moderately

Words & music by Malvina Reynolds

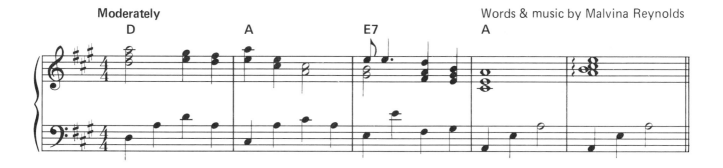

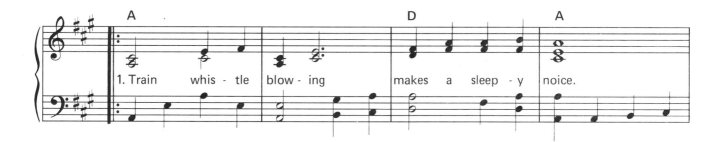

1. Train whis - tle blow - ing makes a sleep - y noice.

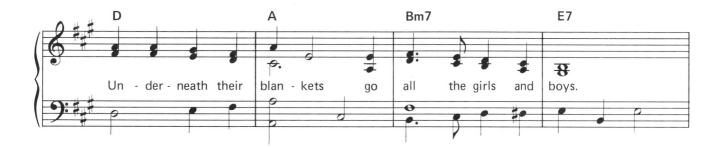

Un - der - neath their blan - kets go all the girls and boys.

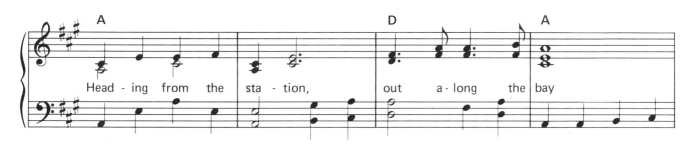

Head - ing from the sta - tion, out a - long the bay

All bound for Morn-ing-town man-y miles a-way.

Ending

2. Sarah's at the engine, Tony rings the bell
   John swings the lantern, to show that all is well
   Rocking, rolling, riding, out along the bay
   All bound for Morningtown, many miles away

3. Maybe it is raining where our train will ride
   But all the little travellers are snug and warm inside
   Somewhere there is sunshine, somewhere there is day
   Somewhere there is Morningtown, many miles away.

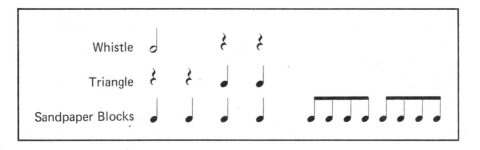

Rise and Shine

Words & Music by Raffi, B. and B. Simpson

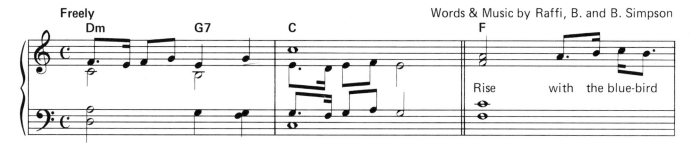

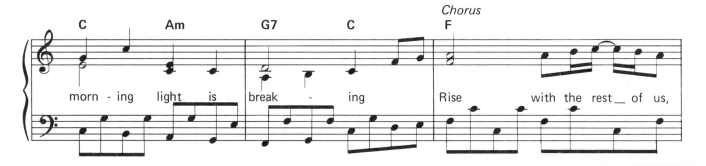

Chorus

morn - ing light is break - ing Rise with the rest __ of us,

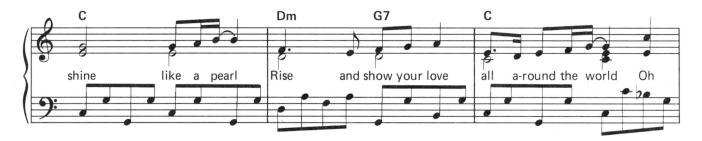

shine like a pearl Rise and show your love all a-round the world Oh

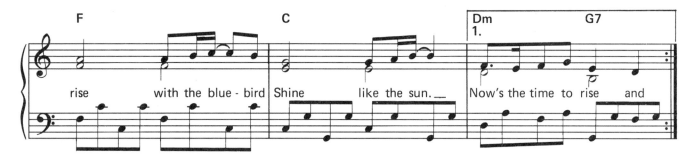

rise with the blue - bird Shine like the sun. __ Now's the time to rise and

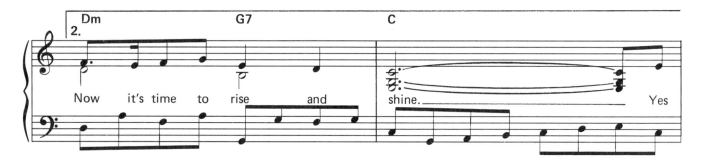

Now it's time to rise and shine. _____ Yes

now's the time to rise and shine.

2. Rise and shine
   Today is calling and
   This is what it's saying.
   Rise and shine
   Your friends are waking
   It's time for work and playing.

Walk, Walk, Walk

Briskly

Words & Music by Raffi

1. I've just had my or-ange juice. I'm put-ting on my walk-ing shoes.

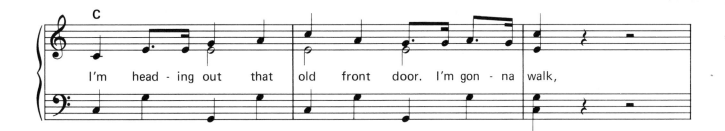

I'm head-ing out that old front door. I'm gon-na walk,

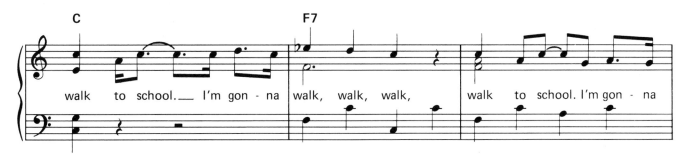

walk to school.__ I'm gon-na walk, walk, walk, walk to school. I'm gon-na

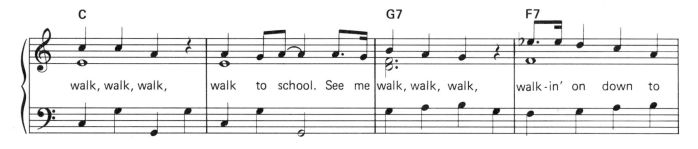

walk, walk, walk, walk to school. See me walk, walk, walk, walk-in' on down to

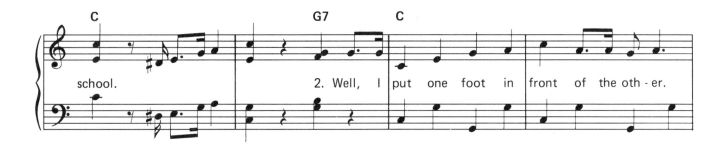

school. 2. Well, I put one foot in front of the oth - er.

Take one step and then an - oth - er. That's how I walk, That's

how I walk, See me walk, walk, walk, walk - in' all 'round the

town. 3. I'm gon - na take my base - ball glove,

I'm gon-na take my skip-ping rope. I'm gon-na call some friends I know, we're gon-na

walk, walk to the park, We're gon - na walk, walk, walk,

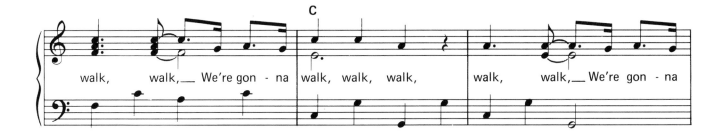

walk, walk,__ We're gon - na walk, walk, walk, walk, walk,__ We're gon - na

walk, walk, walk, walk-in' on down to the park. Well, it's

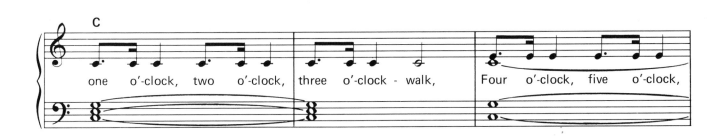

one o'-clock, two o'-clock, three o'-clock - walk, Four o'-clock, five o'-clock,

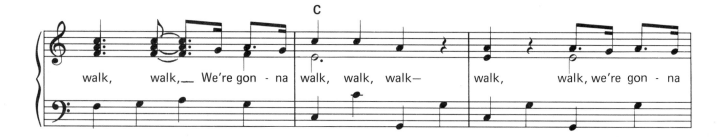

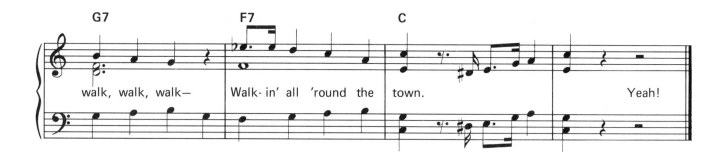

This song can also be played with the capo behind the 3rd fret,
substituting the chords   A | E7 | D7
for   C | G7 | F7

Thumbelina

With a bounce

Words & Music by Frank Loesser

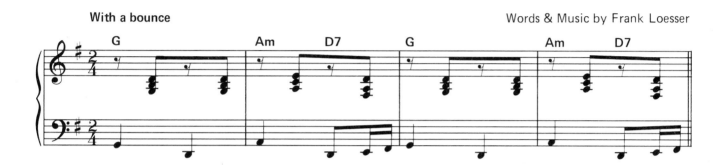

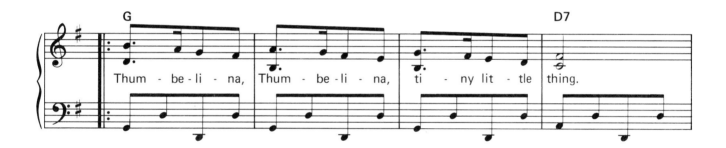

Thum - be - li - na, Thum - be - li - na, ti - ny lit - tle thing.

Thum - be - li - na, dance. Thum - be - li - na sing, Oh

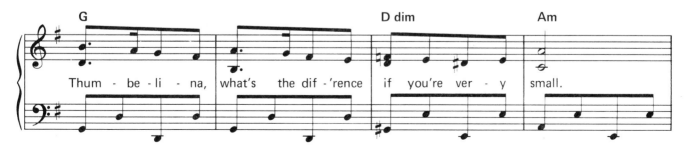

Thum - be - li - na, what's the dif - 'rence if you're ver - y small.

42

To Coda after 3rd repeat

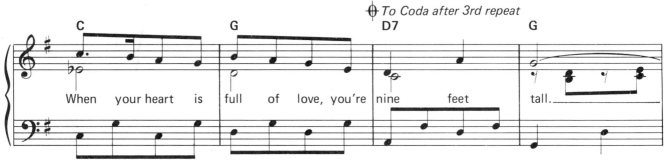

When your heart is full of love, you're nine feet tall.

1. Though you're no big-ger than my

thumb, than my thumb, than my thumb

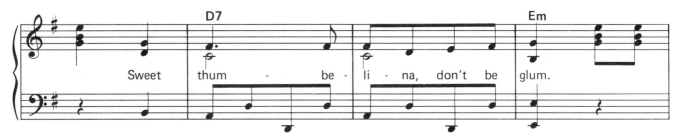

Sweet thum - be - li - na, don't be glum.

Now, now, now, ah, ah, ah, come, come come.

Coda

nine feet tall.

2. Though you're no bigger than my toe
Than my toe, than my toe.

Sweet Thumbelina, keep that glow
And you'll grow, and you'll grow
and you'll grow.

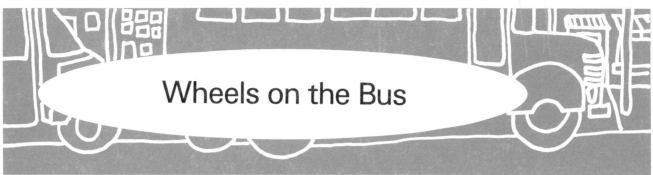

Wheels on the Bus

Moderately

Traditional

Eb

Bb7   Eb

1. The wheels on the bus go

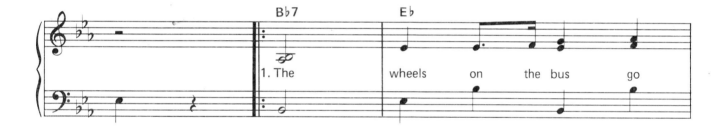

Bb7   Eb

round and round, Round and round, Round and round, The

Bb7

wheels on the bus go round and round, All a - round the

2. The wipers on the bus
Go swish swish swish . . .

3. The driver on the bus
Goes "Move on back!" . . .

4. The people on the bus
Go up and down . . .

5. The horn on the bus
Goes "beep, beep, beep" . . .

6. The baby on the bus
Goes "Wah, wah, wah" . . .

7. The parents on the bus
Go "Shh, shh, shh" . . .

To play this in D, substitute the chords   D | A7
                                       for E♭ | B♭7
The capo behind the 1st fret gives you the Key of E♭; move it to the
2nd fret and you have the Key of E.

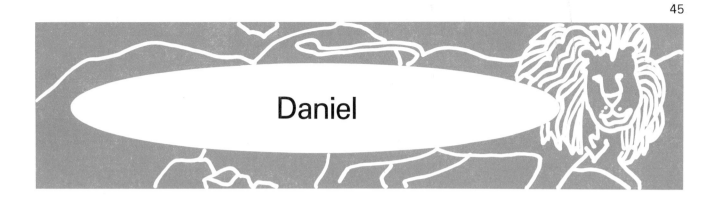

Daniel

Moderately

Trad., adapted by Raffi and Ken Whiteley

1. & 4. Dan - iel in the li - on's den, Dan - iel in the

li - on's den, Dan-iel in the li - on's den. ___

Now _____ is the need - ed time.

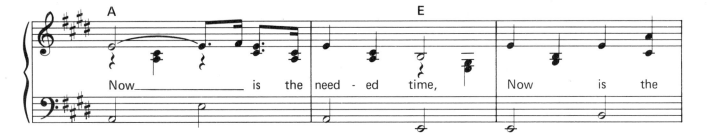

Now_____ is the need - ed time, Now is the

need - ed time.

2. You promised that you'd answer prayer . . .
   Lord, won't you come by here? . . .

3. And then God, he sent an angel down . . .
   And the angel locked the lion's jaw . . .

Five Little Ducks

Brightly   Traditional

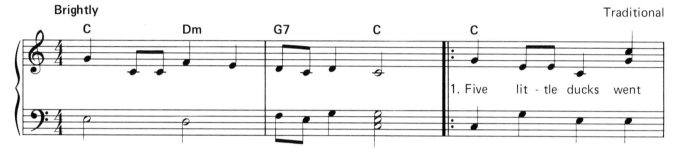

1. Five lit - tle ducks went

out one day   O - ver the hills and   far a - way

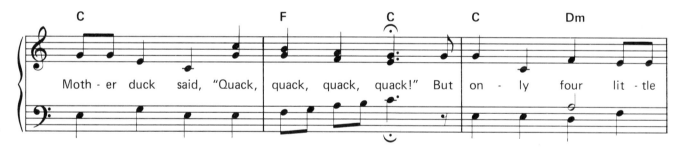

Moth - er duck said, "Quack, quack, quack, quack!" But on - ly four lit - tle

Ending

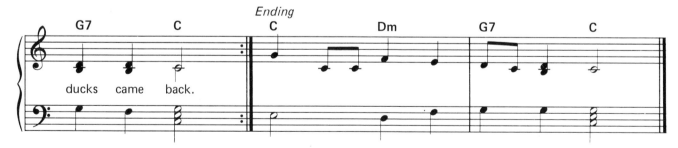

ducks came back.

2. Four little ducks went out one day . . .
   But only three little ducks came back.

3. Three little ducks went out one day . . .
   But only two little ducks came back.

4. Two little ducks went out one day . . .
   But only one little duck came back.

5. One little duck went out one day . . .
   But none of the five little ducks came back.

6. Sad mother duck went out one day . . .
   And all of the five little ducks came back.

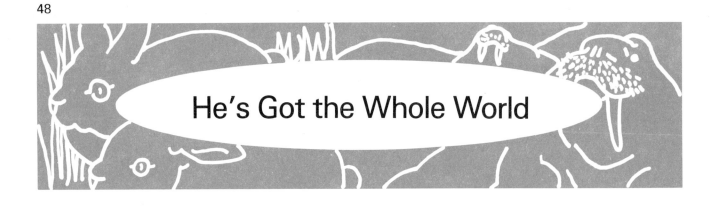

He's Got the Whole World

Trad., adapted by Raffi

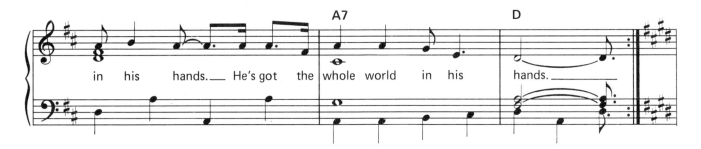

1. He's got my brothers and my sisters . . .
   He's got the whole world in his hands.

2. He's got the little bitty baby . . .
   He's got the whole world in his hands.

3. He's got the birds in the air . . .
   He's got the whales in the sea . . .
   He's got you and he's got me . . .
   He's got the whole world in his hands.

Verse 4 and Refrain

4. He's got ev - 'ry-bod - y here___ in his hands. He's got

ev - 'ry-bod - y here___ in his hands. He's got ___ ev - 'ry-bod - y here___

in his hands. He's got the whole world in his hands.___

Hand Claps   (for Chorus only)

Big Beautiful Planet

Moderately, with feeling

Words & Music by Raffi

Chorus

There's a big beauti-ful plan-et in the sky, _____ And it's my

home _____ It's where I live. You and man-y oth-ers live here

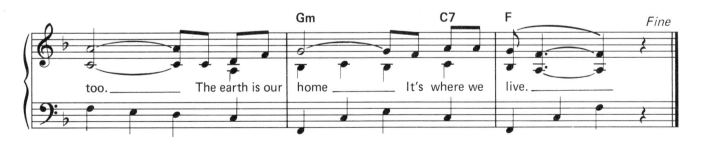

too. _____ The earth is our home _____ It's where we live. _____

Fine

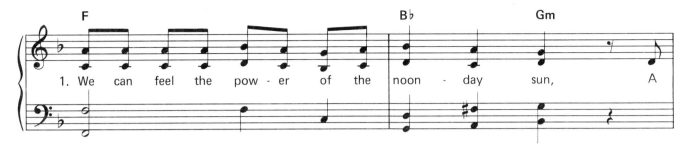

1. We can feel the pow-er of the noon-day sun, A

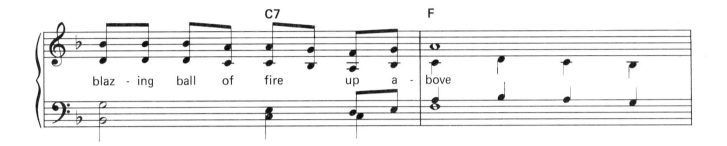

blaz-ing ball of fire up a-bove

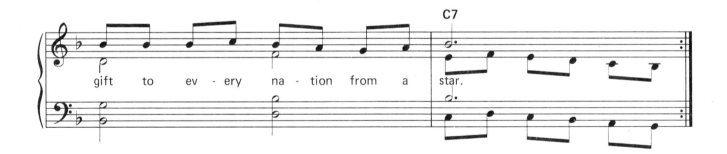

Shin-ing light and warmth e-nough for ev-ery-one, A

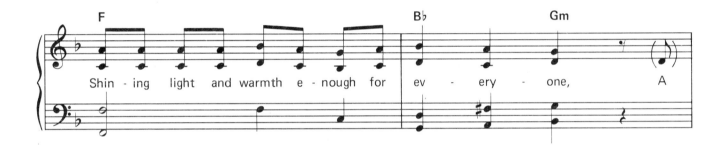

gift to ev-ery na-tion from a star.

2. We can feel the spirit of a blowing wind
   A mighty source of power in our lives.
   Offering another way to fill our needs,
   Nature's gift to help us carry on.

Raffi plays this with the capo behind the 1st fret, substituting

the chords

E	F♯m	B7	A
F	Gm	C7	B♭

I'm in the Mood

With gusto

Words & Music by Raffi

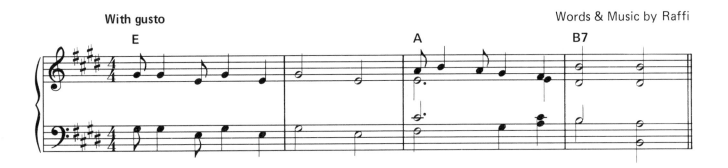

1. I'm in the mood for sing - ing. Hey, how a-bout you?

I'm in the mood for sing - ing. Hey, how a- bout you?

I'm in the mood for sing - ing, Sing-ing a - long with you.

Hey, hey, what do you say? I'm in the mood for that to-day.

Hey, hey, what do you say? I'm in the mood for that.

2. I'm in the mood for clapping . . .

3. I'm in the mood for whistling . . .

4. I'm in the mood for stomp - ing... Hey, how a-bout

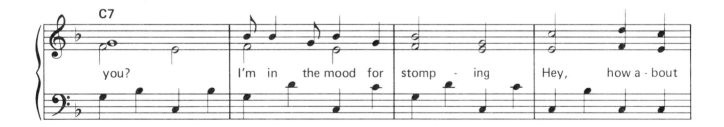

you? I'm in the mood for stomp - ing Hey, how a - bout

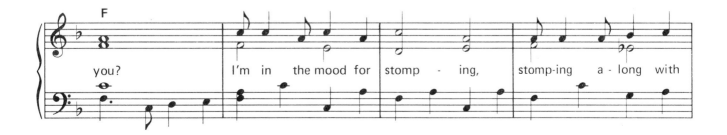

you? I'm in the mood for stomp - ing, stomp-ing a - long with

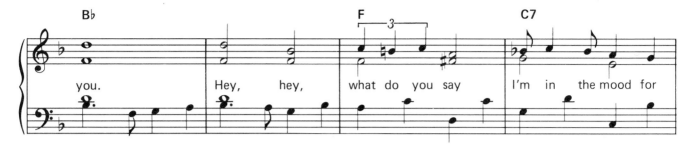

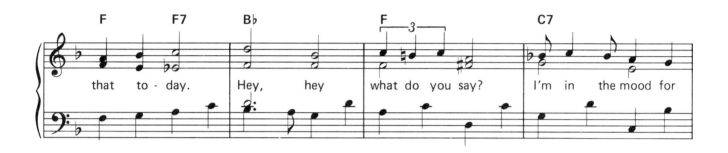

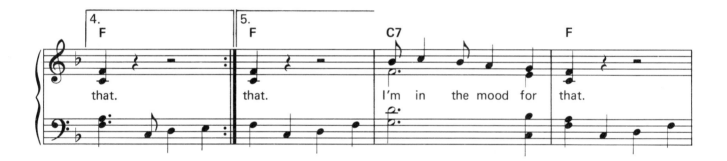

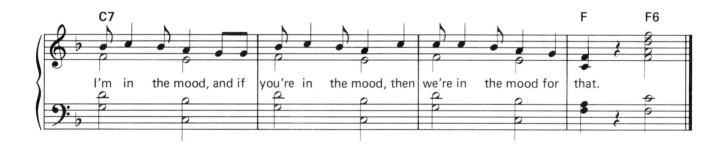

5. I'm in the mood for singing . . .

Something in My Shoe

Briskly

Words & Music by Al Simmons

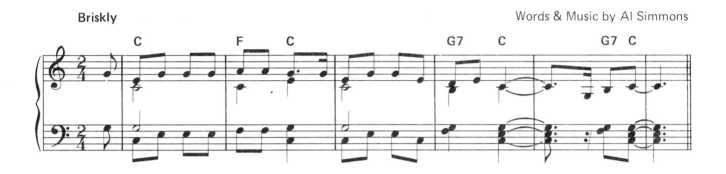

1. As I was going out for a walk I got no further than half a block

Trou-ble with my foot. Ooh, there was some-thing in my shoe So I

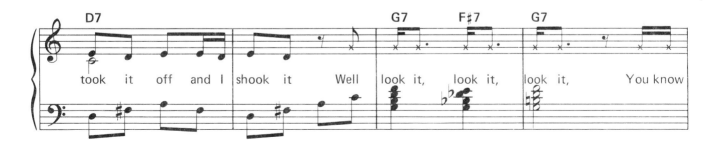

took it off and I shook it Well look it, look it, look it, You know

56

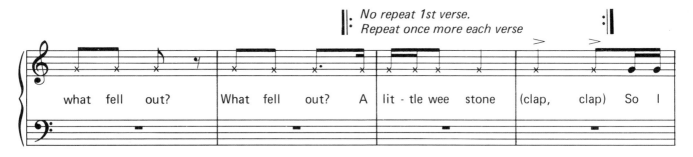

No repeat 1st verse.
Repeat once more each verse

what fell out? What fell out? A lit-tle wee stone (clap, clap) So I

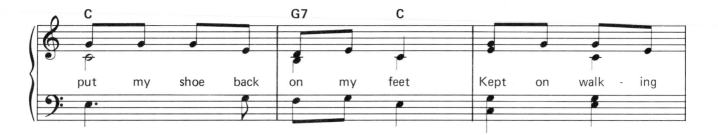

put my shoe back on my feet Kept on walk - ing

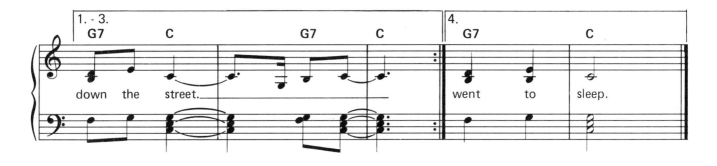

down the street._____ went to sleep.

2. As I was going to the store
   One step, two step, three step, four
   Trouble with my foot
   Ooh, there was something in my shoe
   So I took it off and I shook it
   Now look it, look it, look it.
   You know what fell out? (What fell out?)
   A bouncing ball (boing, boing)
   And a little wee stone (clap, clap)
   So I put my shoe back on my feet,
   Kept on walking down the street.

3. As I was driving in my car
   I couldn't drive very far
   Trouble with my foot . . . (What fell out?)
   A flying bird (tweet, tweet)
   A bouncing ball (boing, boing)
   A little wee stone (clap, clap)

4. I went home and stood on the kitchen floor
   I didn't think I'd have any more
   Trouble with my foot . . . (What fell out?)
   A locomotive (toot, toot)
   A flying bird (tweet, tweet)
   A bouncing ball (boing, boing)
   A little wee stone (clap, clap)
   So I went to my room in bare feet
   Climbed into bed and went to sleep.

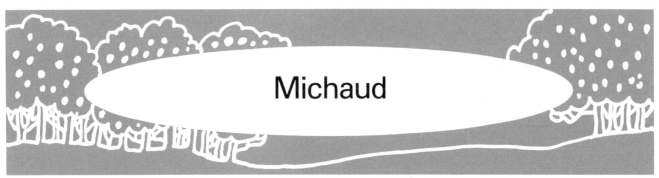

Michaud

Lightly

Trad., adapted by Raffi and Lise Poitras

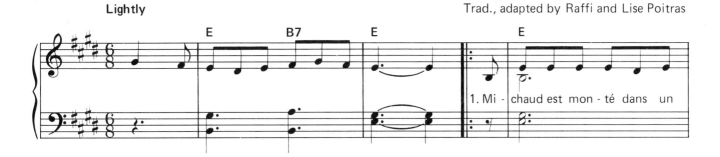

1. Mi - chaud est mon - té dans un

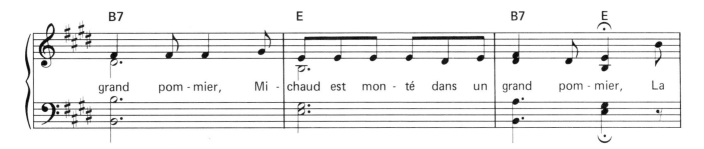

grand pom - mier, Mi - chaud est mon - té dans un grand pom - mier, La

branche s'est sée. crack! Mi - chaud est tom - bé BOOM! Où

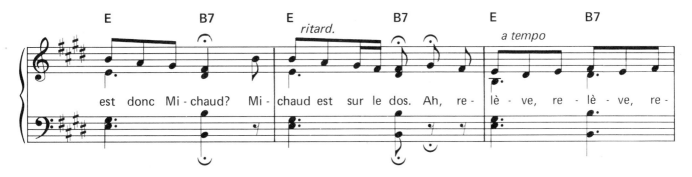

ritard.   *a tempo*

est donc Mi - chaud? Mi - chaud est sur le dos. Ah, re - lè - ve, re - lè - ve, re -

lè - ve, Ah, re - lè - ve, re - lè - ve, Mi - chaud.

4. Mi - chaud est re - mon - té dans le grand pom - mier. Il a trouvé

une pomme et crunch!

2. Michaud est monté dans un grand pêcher . . .

3. Michaud est monté dans un cerisier . . .

Instrument sounds for noises in the song
CRACK - Hit two flat pieces of wood together
BOOM - One hit on a drum

Tête, Epaules

March Traditional

Tête, é - paules, ge - noux et pieds, ge - noux et pieds, Tête, é - paules, ge - noux et pieds, ge - noux et pieds J'ai un nez, deux yeux, deux o - reilles, et une bouche. Tête, é - paules, ge - noux et pieds, ge - noux et pieds.

2. Head and shoulders, knees and feet, knees and feet,
Head and shoulders, knees and feet, knees and feet,
I've a nose, two eyes, two ears, and a mouth
Head and shoulders, knees and feet, knees and feet.

Let's Do the Numbers Rumba

Latin feel

Words & music by David Walden

Chorus

(Spoken) One, two, three, four:

Let's do the num - bers

rum - ba.   Let's do the num - bers   rum - ba.

Let's do the num - bers   rum - ba.   Num - bers rum - ba all   day

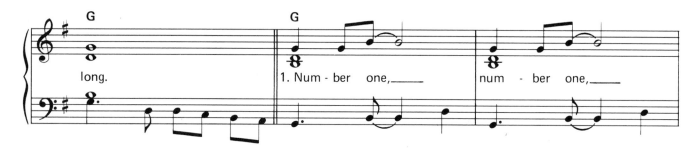

long.   1. Num - ber   one,_____   num - ber one,_____

2. Number two, number two
   Two big feet on a kangaroo.
   Number two, number two
   Number two all day long.

3. Number three, number three
   Three bananas on banana tree.
   Number three, number three
   Number three all day long.

Last ending for Chorus

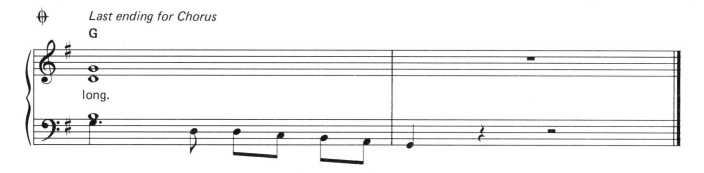

long.

Try the maracas or claves (woodblocks) and play the rhythm you feel.

Ducks Like Rain

Words & music by Franciscus Henri

Moderately

Quack,   quack quack quack quack

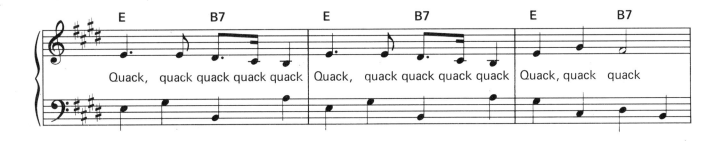

Quack,   quack quack quack quack   Quack,   quack quack quack quack   Quack, quack   quack

Quack, quack quack quack quack   Quack, quack quack quack quack   Quack, quack quack quack quack

quack quack quack.   1. Ducks like   rain,   Ducks like   rain,   Ducks like splish-ing splash-ing

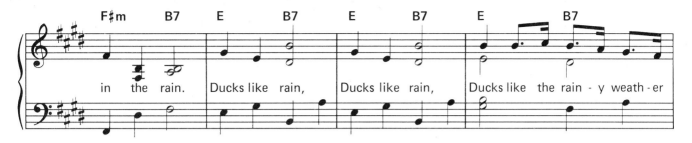

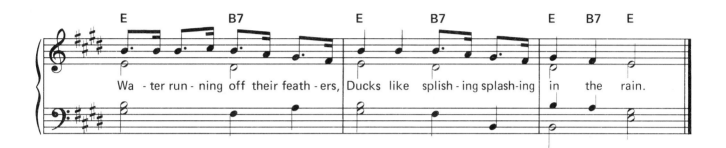

2. Quack, quack quack . . .
Ducks like rain, ducks like rain
Ducks like to widdle, waddle in the rain.
Ducks like rain, ducks like rain
Ducks like to widdle, waddle
Water knee-deep in the puddle
Ducks like to widdle, waddle in the rain.

Row, Row, Row

Traditional

Dreamily

C   G7   C   *Fine*

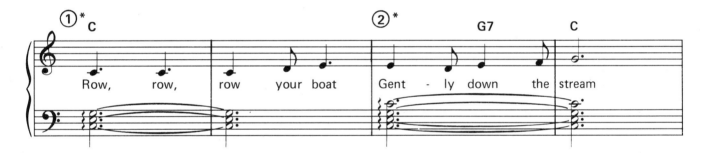

① * C   ② *   G7   C

Row,   row,   row   your boat   Gent - ly down the stream

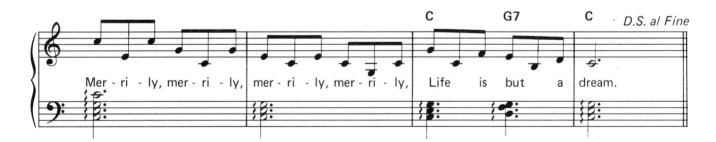

C   G7   C   *D.S. al Fine*

Mer - ri - ly, mer - ri - ly, mer - ri - ly, mer - ri - ly, Life   is   but   a   dream.

Descant

No. 1 and 2 — for entry when sung as a round.

This Little Light of Mine

Spirited

Trad., adapted by Raffi

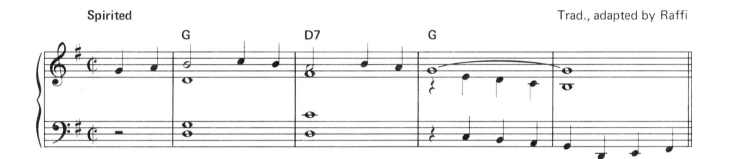

Chorus

This lit-tle light of mine. I'm gon-na let it shine.

This lit-tle light of mine. I'm gon-na let it shine.

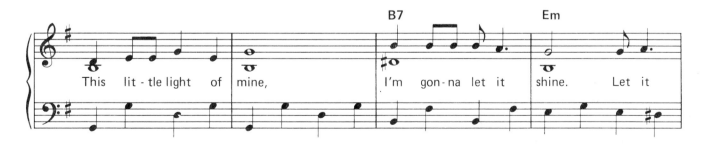

This lit-tle light of mine, I'm gon-na let it shine. Let it

Last time to Coda

shine, let it shine, Let it shine. 1. I'm gon-na

take this light a-round the world And I'm gon-na let it shine. I'm gon-na

take this light a-round the world, And I'm gon-na let it shine. I'm gon-na

take this light a-round the world, And I'm gon-na let it shine, Let it

shine, let it shine, Let it shine.

Coda

Ev-'ry day,___ ev-'ry day.___ I'm gon-na let my lit-tle light shine.

2. I won't let anyone (blow) it out   I'm gonna let it shine
    I won't let anyone (blow) it out   Let it shine, let it shine, let it shine.
    I won't let anyone (blow) it out

Time to Sing

Words & music by Raffi,
D. Pike and B. & B. Simpson

Happily

1. It's

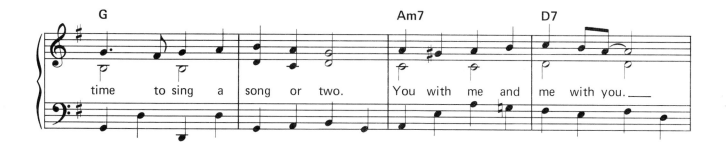

time to sing a song or two. You with me and me with you.____

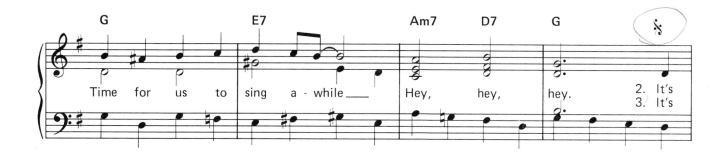

Time for us to sing a - while____ Hey, hey, hey.

2. It's
3. It's

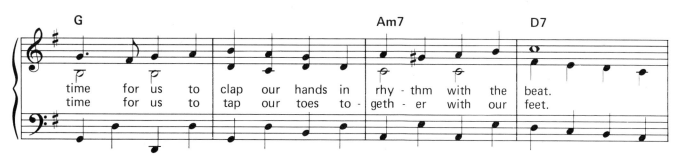

time for us to clap our hands in rhy - thm with the beat.
time for us to tap our toes to - geth - er with our feet.

G   E7   Am7 D7   G   *Chorus*

Time for hands to   clap a - while ___ Hey, hey   hey.   And it's
Time for toes to   tap a - while ___ Hey, hey   hey.

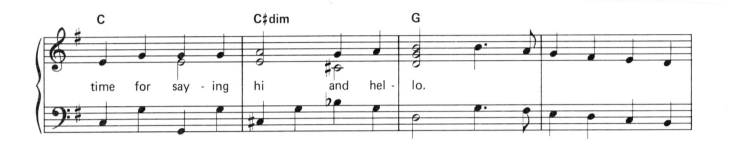

C   C#dim   G

time for say - ing hi   and hel - lo.

A7   D7   *(After Verse 3 to Coda)* *D.S.*

Let's all sing a song that we know.

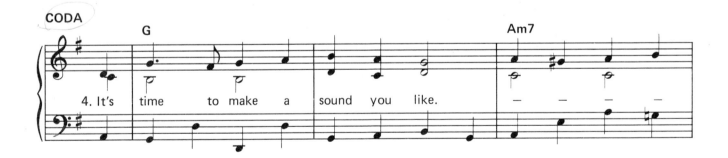

CODA   G   Am7

4. It's time to make a sound you like. — — — —

D7   G   E7   Am7 D7

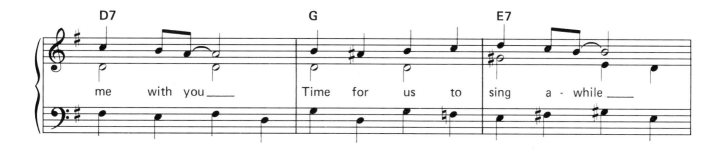

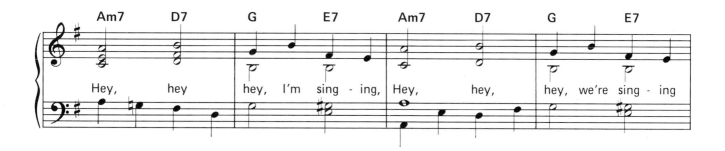

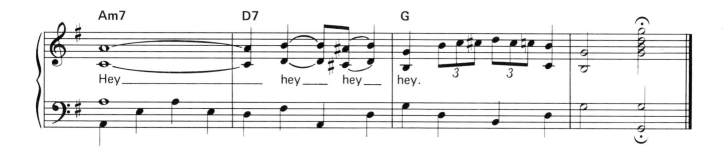

Apples and Bananas

With a bounce

Traditional

1. I like to eat, eat, eat ap - ples and ba - nan - as.

I like to eat, eat, eat ap - ples and ba - nan - as

2. I like to ate . . . aypuls and banaynays.

3. I like to eet . . . eeples and baneenees.

4. I like to ite . . . iples and baninis.

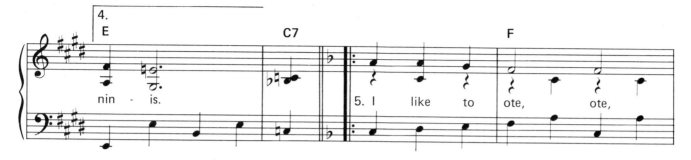

6. I like to ute . . . uples and banunus.

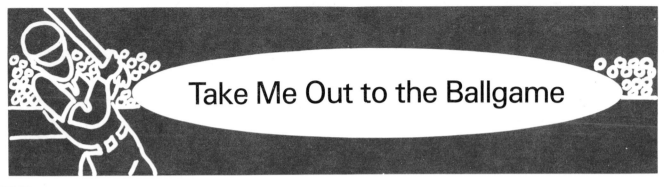

Take Me Out to the Ballgame

Words & music by
Harry von Tilzer and Jack Norworth

Take me

out to the ball game. Take me out with the

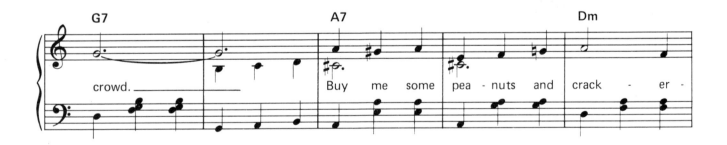

crowd. Buy me some pea - nuts and crack - er -

jack. I don't care if I nev - er come back. With a

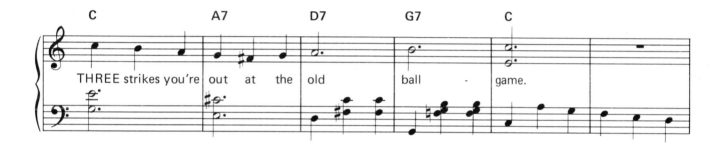

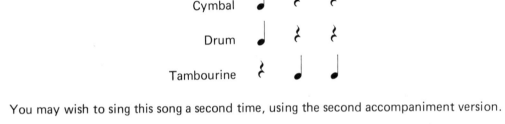

You may wish to sing this song a second time, using the second accompaniment version.

Octopus's Garden

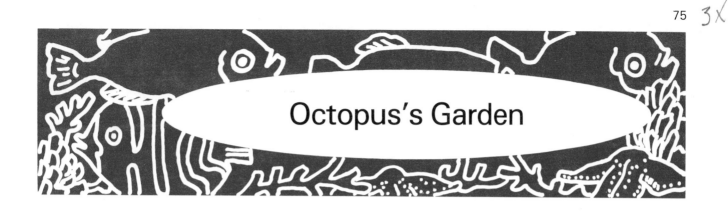

Brightly

Words & music by Richard Starkey

C   Am   F   G

C   Am

1. I'd like to be ____   un-der the sea,   In an

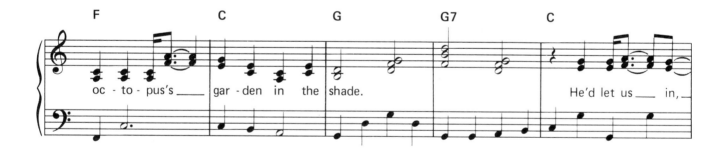

F   C   G   G7   C

oc-to-pus's ____ gar-den in the shade.   He'd let us ____ in,

     Am   F

____   Knows where we've been   In his oc-to-pus's ____

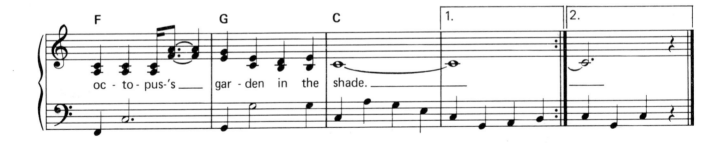

2. We would be warm, below the storm
   In our little hideaway beneath the waves,
   Resting our heads, on the sea bed.
   In an octopus's garden near a cave.
   We would sing and dance around,
   Because we know we can't be found.
   I'd like to be under the sea
   In an octopus's garden in the shade.

Fais Dodo

Gently

French Traditional

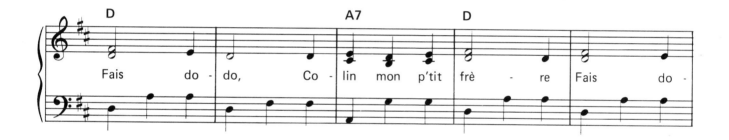

Fais do - do, Co - lin mon p'tit frè - re Fais do -

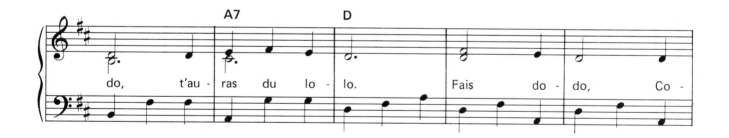

do, t'au - ras du lo - lo. Fais do - do, Co -

lin, mon p'tit frè - re. Fais do - do, t'au - ras du lo - lo.

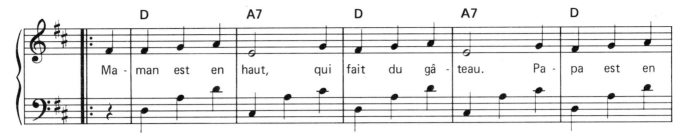

Ma - man est en haut, qui fait du gâ - teau. Pa - pa est en

bas, qui fait du cho - co - lat.   Fais   do -

do,   Co - lin, mon p'tit frè - re.   Fais   do - do,   t'au -

For 2nd ending go to Coda

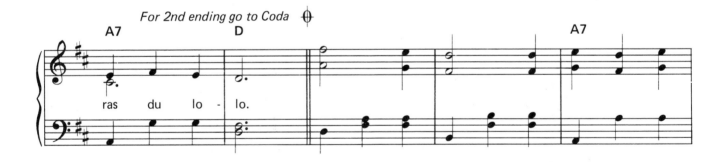

ras du lo - lo.

CODA

Fine

In My Garden

Words & music by
Alan Arkin and Jeremy Arkin

Sprightly

1. Dig - ging, dig - ging, This is how we dig the ground

In our gar - den, in our gar - den. Dig - ging, dig - ging, This is how we dig the ground

Ear - ly in the morn - ing ____ 3. Plant - ing, plant - ing,

This is how we plant the seeds In our gar - den, in our gar - den Plant - ing plant - ing

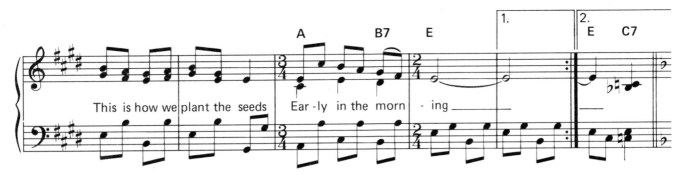

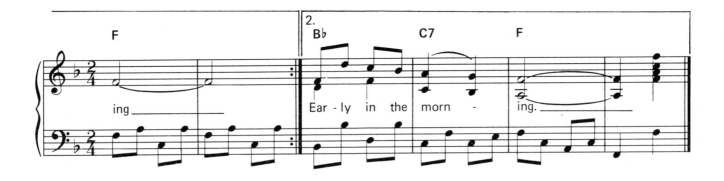

2. Hoeing, hoeing
   This is how we hoe the weeds . . .

4. Growing, growing
   This is how the peas will grow . . .

6. Eating, eating
   This is how we'll eat the peas
   From our garden . . .

Riding in an Airplane

Words & music by Raffi,
D. Pike, B. & B. Simpson

Refrain

Rid - ing in an air - plane _____ High a - bove the ground. _____

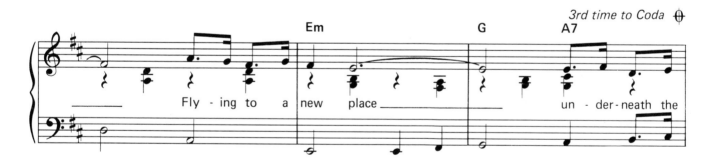

3rd time to Coda

Fly - ing to a new place _____ un - der - neath the

sun.

1. Look - ing out my win - dow _____
2. The lights of the cit - y _____

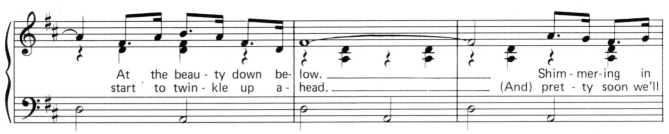

At the beau - ty down be - low. _____ Shim - mer-ing in
start to twin - kle up a - head. _____ (And) pret - ty soon we'll

Em   G   A7   D   *2nd time go to* *

sun - light _____ I see the riv - ers on the go. _____
touch down _____ just be - fore it's time for bed. _____

Bm

_____ 2. Choc- 'late col - oured farms _____ with the food the far - mer

D   Em

grows _____ Wait - ing for a rain - cloud _____

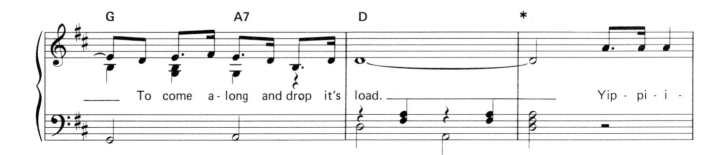

G   A7   D   *

To come a - long and drop it's load. _____ Yip - pi - i -

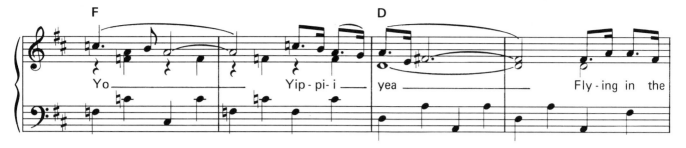

Yo ___ Yip-pi-i ___ yea ___ Fly-ing in the

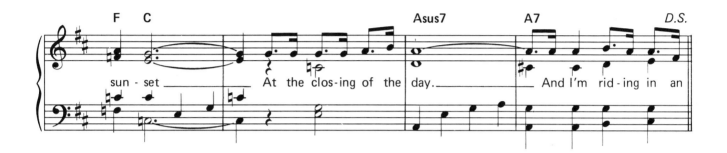

sun-set ___ At the clos-ing of the day. ___ And I'm rid-ing in an

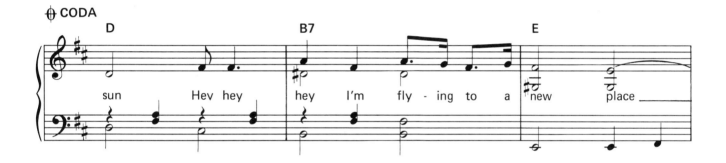

CODA

sun Hey hey hey I'm fly-ing to a new place ___

___ un-der-neath the sun Whoa ___ un-der-neath the

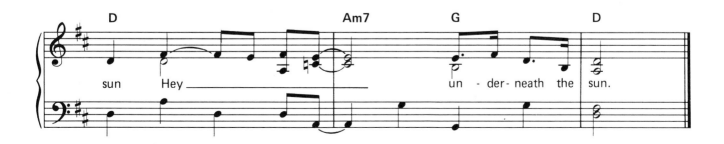

sun Hey ___ un-der-neath the sun.

Like Me and You

Moderately, with feeling

Words & music by Raffi, D. Pike

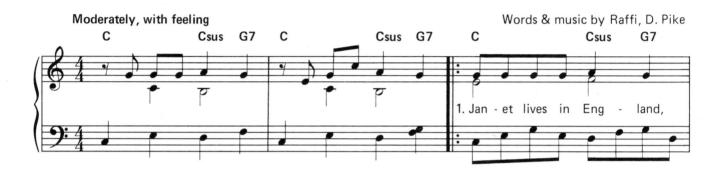

1. Jan-et lives in Eng - land,

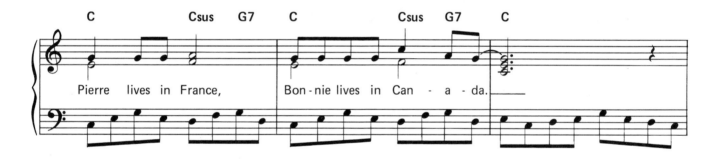

Pierre lives in France, Bon-nie lives in Can - a - da.

Ah-med lives in E - gypt, Mo-she lives in Is-ra-el. Bruce lives in Aus-tra - li - a.

Ching lives in Chi - na

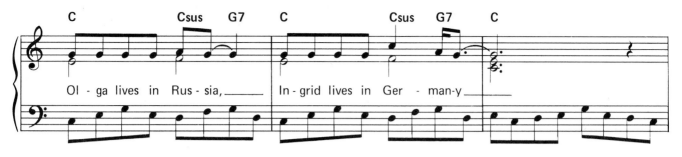

Olga lives in Russia, Ingrid lives in Germany

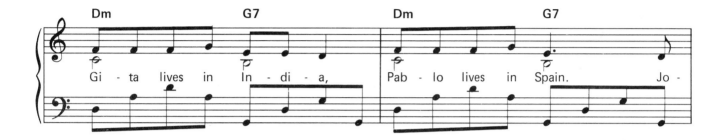

Gita lives in India, Pablo lives in Spain. Jo-

sé lives in Colombia.

Chorus

And each one is much like another. A child of a mother and a

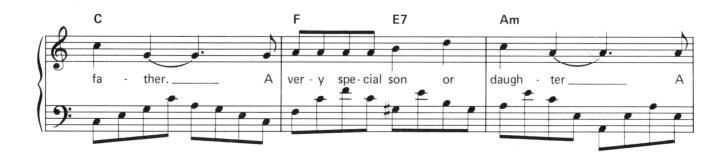

father. A very special son or daughter A

F   G7

lot   like me and   you.

CODA

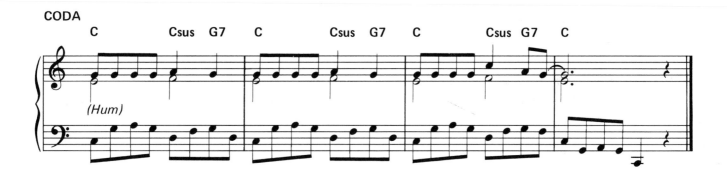

C   Csus G7   C   Csus G7   C   Csus G7   C

(Hum)

2. Koji lives in Japan, Nina lives in Chile
   Farida lives in Pakistan.
   Zosia lives in Poland, Manuel lives in Brazil
   Maria lives in Italy.
   Kofi lives in Ghana, Rahim lives in Iran
   Rosa lives in Paraguay.
   Meja lives in Kenya, Demetri lives in Greece
   Sue lives in America.

This song is played with the capo behind the 3rd fret,
substituting the chords

A	Asus	E7	Bm	D	Adim	C♯7	F♯m

for

C	Csus	G7	Dm	F	Cdim	E7	Am

Triangle

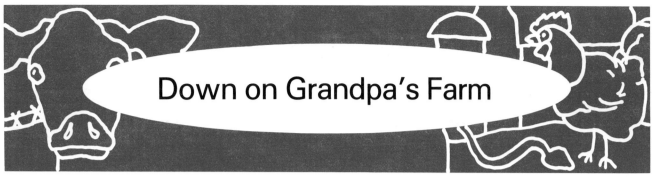

Down on Grandpa's Farm

With gusto

Traditional

Chorus

Oh we're on our way, we're on our way, on our way to Grand-pa's

farm We're on our way, We're on our way, on our

way to Grand-pa's farm. _____ farm.

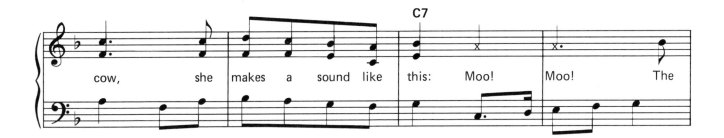

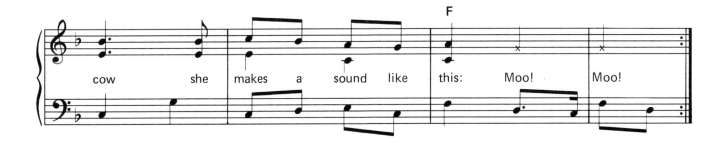

2. Down on Grandpa's farm there is a little red hen.

3. Down on Grandpa's farm there is a little white sheep.

4. Down on Grandpa's farm there is a big black dog.

5. Down on Grandpa's farm there is a big brown horse.

You may elect to play this with the chords **E** and **B7**, capo as needed.

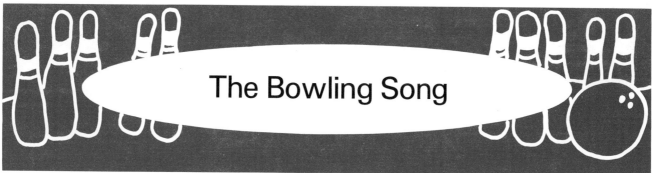

The Bowling Song

Words & music by Raffi
D. Pike, B. and B. Simpson

I like to go bowl-ing with my friend Bert, My bowl-ing ball and my

bowl-ing shirt. I like to roll the ball___ down the lane___

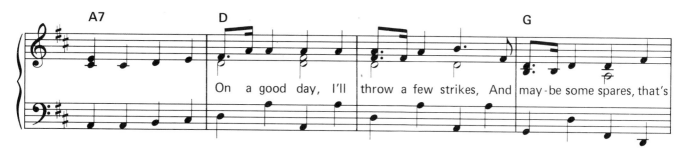

On a good day, I'll throw a few strikes, And may-be some spares, that's

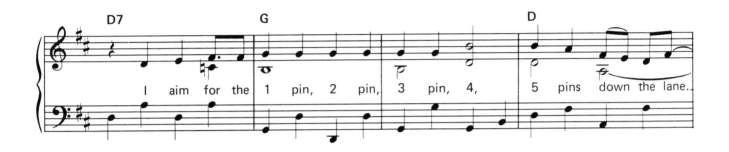

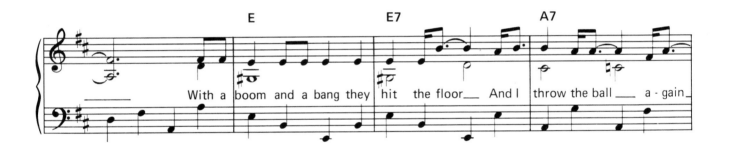

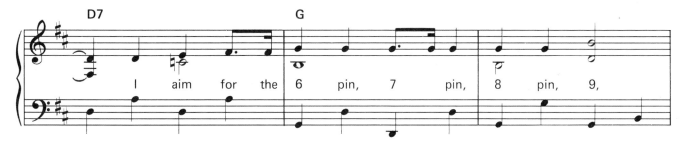

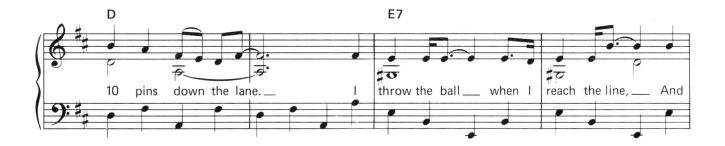

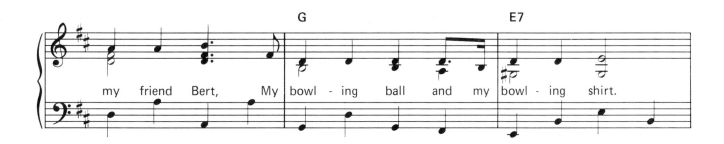

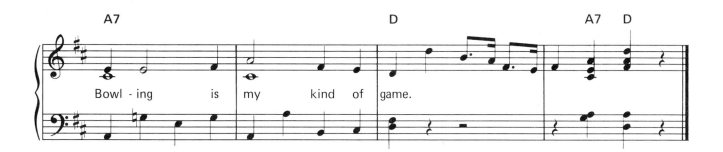

Tingalayo

Trad., adapted by Raffi

Calypso

Chorus

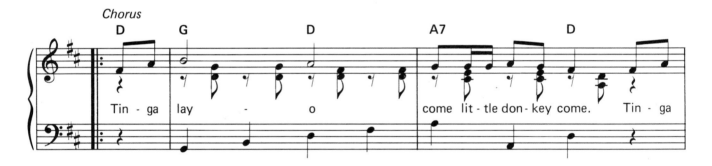

Tin - ga lay - o   come lit - tle don - key come.   Tin - ga

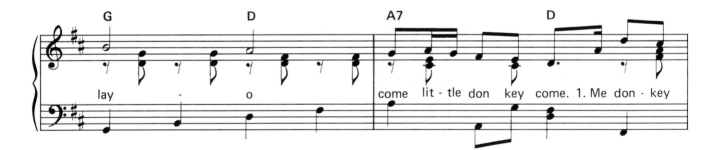

lay - o   come lit - tle don key come. 1. Me don - key

fast,   me don - key slow,   Me don - key come and   me don - key go.   Me don - key

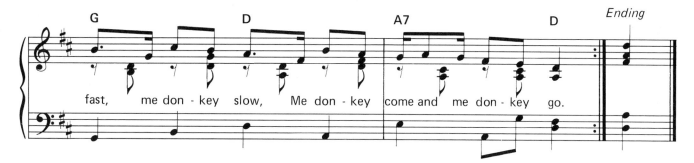

fast, me don - key slow, Me don - key come and me don - key go.

2. Me donkey hee, me donkey haw,
   Me donkey sleep in a bed of straw.

3. Me donkey dance, me donkey sing,
   Me donkey wearin' a diamond ring.

4. Me donkey swim, me donkey ski,
   Me donkey dress elegantly.

Walk Outside

Briskly

Words & music by Dick Tarrier

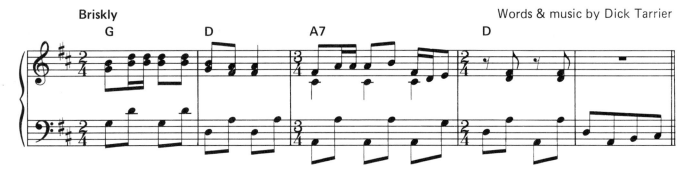

Chorus

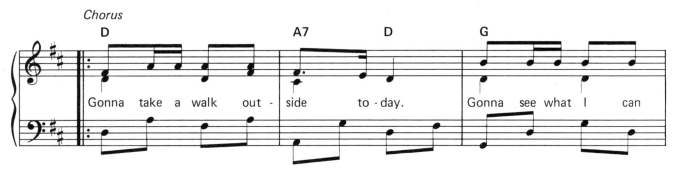

Gonna take a walk out - side to-day. Gonna see what I can

find to - day. Gonna take a walk out - side to-day. I'm

Last Chorus to Coda

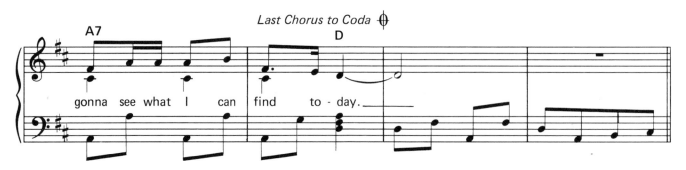

gonna see what I can find to - day.

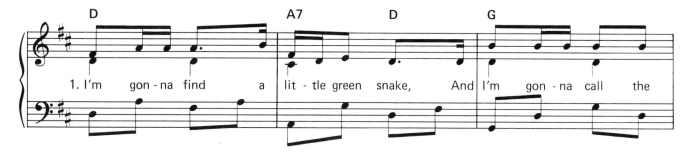

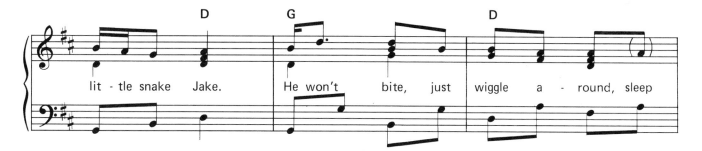

2. I'm gonna find a little grey squirrel
   And I'm gonna call the little squirrel Earl.
   He can jump from limb to limb
   Don't I wish I could jump like him.

3. I'm gonna find a little lost pup
   And I'm gonna pick the little pup up.
   I ll take him home, he'll be my pal
   He'll chase sticks, I'll call him Hal.

4. I'm gonna find a little lost duck
   And I'm gonna call the little duck Chuck.
   He can live in the pond out back.
   Swim all day and go "quack quack quack."

De Colores

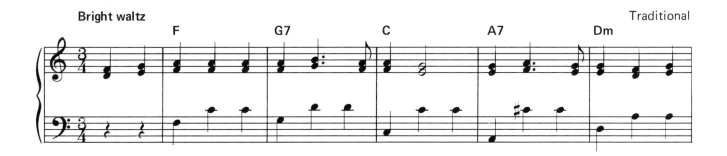

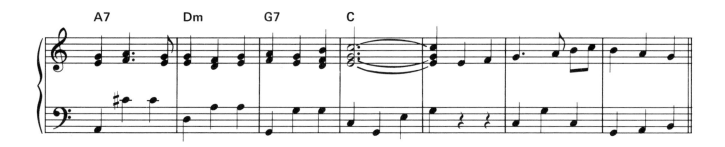

De _____ co - lo - res,   De co - lo - res se vis - ten los

G7

cam - pos En la pri - ma - ve - ra.

G7

De _____ co - lo - res. De co - lo - res son los par - jar -

C

i - tos Que vie - nen de a - fuer a._____

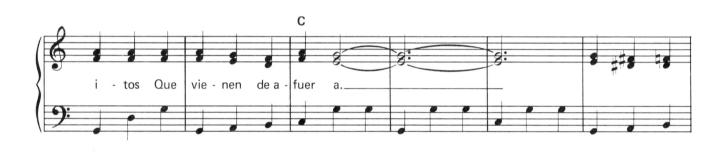

C

De _____ co - lo - res De co - lo - res es el ar - co

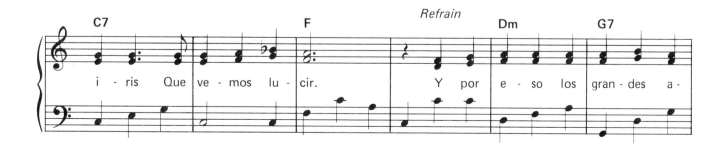

C7

F

Refrain

Dm

G7

i - ris Que ve - mos lu - cir. Y por e - so los gran - des a -

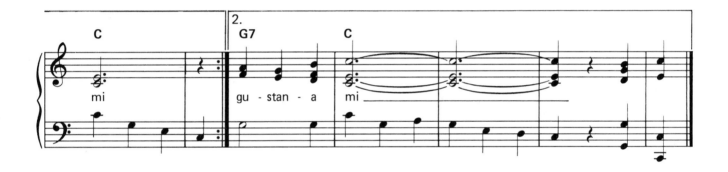

2. Canta el gallo
   Canta el gallo con el quiri, quiri
   Quiri, quiri quiri
   La gallina,
   La gallina con el cara, cara
   Cara, cara, cara
   Los polluelos,
   Los polluelos con el pio, pio
   Pio, pio, pio.

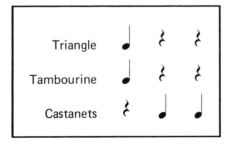

Twinkle, Twinkle, Little Star

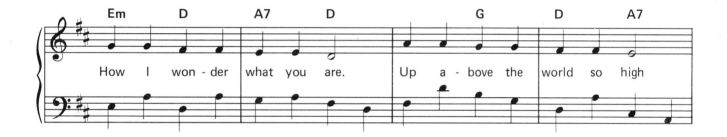

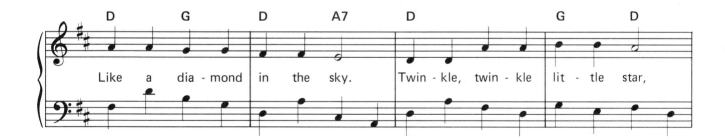

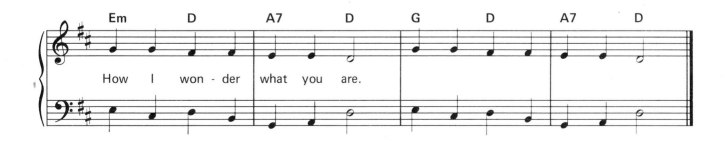

One Light, One Sun

Flowing

Words & music by Raffi

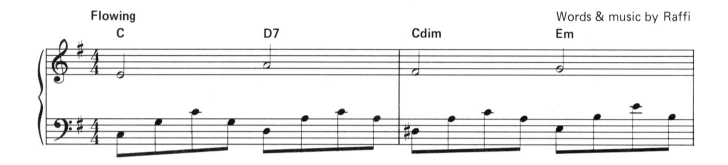

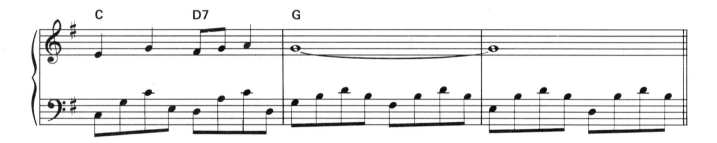

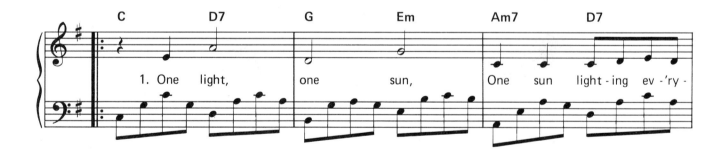

1. One light, one sun, One sun light-ing ev-'ry-one. One world turn-ing

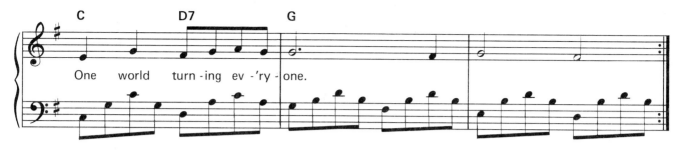

One world turn-ing ev-'ry-one.

CODA

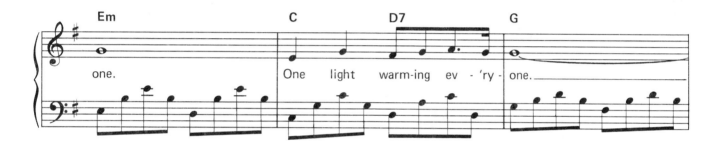

One light, one sun, One sun light-ing ev-'ry-

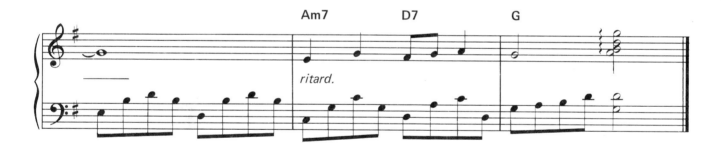

one. One light warm-ing ev-'ry-one.

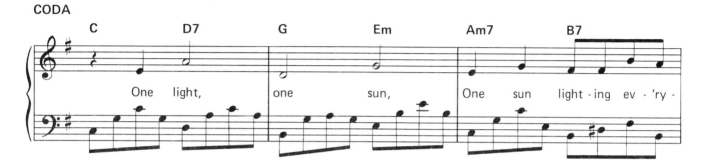

ritard.

2. One world, one home
   One world home for everyone
   One dream, one song
   One song heard by everyone.

3. One love, one heart
   One heart warming everyone
   One hope, one joy
   One love filling everyone.

Triangle

A NOTE TO KEYBOARD PLAYERS

The accompaniments for the songs in this book have been written with simplicity in mind. Where the music appears more difficult, it is often the rhythmic nature of the song that dictates its written form. Listen to the song on the record and catch the rhythm before you start to read the music for it.

In some songs, a second or third verse will have a different accompaniment. This provides variety and allows the accompanist to choose a setting he or she may prefer to use throughout the entire song.

A LITTLE EXTRA - Adding Rhythm Instruments

Some songs in the book have suggestions for rhythmic accompaniment, using rhythm instruments found in schools and some homes. The sounds of these instruments add extra colour to the songs. Feel free to create your own rhythms and experiment with different combinations of rhythm instruments.

A NOTE TO GUITAR PLAYERS

Some songs include suggestions for easy accompaniments as well as Raffi's personal approach. Most comments appear at the end of a given song (look for the 🎸 symbol), with the exception of the following song:

BISCUITS IN THE OVEN

Bill Russell taught Raffi to play this in the Key of A - this is to be done by

substituting the chords

A	A7	D	Adim	E7
for				
C	C7	F	Cdim	G7

Using a capo will raise the pitch as needed for singing. The capo behind the 3rd fret with the "A" chords means you play in the actual Key of C.

GUITAR CHORDS

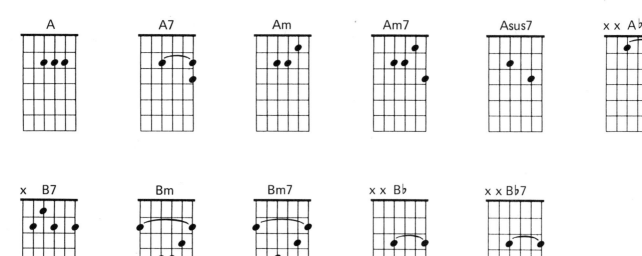

x C   x C7   Csus   x x Cdim

x C#7   C#m   x x C#dim

x D   x D7   x Dm   x x Ddim   x Dm7   x x D#dim

E   E7   Em   x Eb

F   F7   F#7   F#m

G   G7   Gm

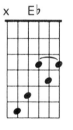

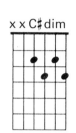
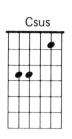
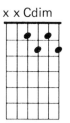

INDEX

All I Really Need   23
Apples and Bananas   70
Baby Beluga   7
Big Beautiful Planet   50
Biscuits in the Oven   9
The Bowling Song   89
Daniel   45
Day O   15
De Colores   96
Down on Grandpa's Farm   87
Ducks Like Rain   62
Fais Dodo   77
Five Little Ducks   47
He's Got the Whole World   48
I'm in the Mood   52
In My Garden   79
Kumbaya   31
Let's Do the Numbers Rumba   60
Like Me and You   84
Michaud   57
Morningtown Ride   33
Oats and Beans and Barley   13
Octopus's Garden   75
One Light, One Sun   100
Over in the Meadow   27
Riding in an Airplane   81
Rise and Shine   35
Row, Row, Row   64
Something in My Shoe   55
Take Me Out to the Ballgame   72
Tête, Epaules...   59
Thanks A Lot   19
This Little Light of Mine   65
This Old Man   29
Thumbelina   41
Time to Sing   67
Tingalayo   92
To Everyone in All the World   21
Twinkle, Twinkle Little Star   99
Walk Outside   94
Walk, Walk, Walk   37
Wheels on the Bus   43